The
Essential
Kathryn Kay

Poems of a Lifetime

The
Essential
Kathryn Kay

Poems of a Lifetime

Compiled by Sheralyn Pratt

Cover Design: Sheralyn Pratt
Illustrations: Plot

ISBN : 978-0-9743331-6-8

First Published, Nov 21, 2020

10 9 8 7 6 5 4 3

Introduction

Kathryn Kay was the twentieth-century poet who claimed:

> *The one thing I'll never say at death's door is:*
> *"I wish I would have..."*
> *for I will have done it all.*

She lived up to her word.

Kathryn Kay was many things before she became my grandma. She was born in 1906 in Salt Lake City, Utah. At the age of 21, she dropped out of college to accept a dream job offer in Hollywood.

Over the next 15 years, Kathryn followed one rule in her career:

Find a job you would pay to do and get paid to do it.

This mantra led her to become:
- The hostess of the Midnight Frolic (the job she left college for), becoming a radio

hostess known as "the Kay who put the 'K' into KFI"
- Personal Representative for P.K. Wrigley
- Event Coordinator for Catalina Island
- Publication Manager for a city magazine
- Associate Editor for the launch of PARADE magazine (while also writing under several pseudonyms to make it look like they had a staff larger than 5 people)
- Business owner of a poetry shop on Olvera Street in Old Los Angeles where she wrote poems and made cards, often for celebrities

Kathryn Kay was well-known enough in her glory days that she once received an overseas letter that was addressed simply to:

Kathryn Kay
U.S.A.

She was always a bit humbled and amazed by the fact that letter ever found her. Yet she hosted a night show on a national radio show interviewing celebrities, so it's not too hard for the modern mind to imagine how such a letter might have found its way to the correct city and person.

Between 1938 and 1944, Kathryn published her three books of poetry before transitioning to private life and raising a family in her hometown of Salt Lake City.

Back in the suburbs, Kathryn focused on building and supporting community programs, including the Art Barn Poets, League of Utah Writers, Utah Press Women, Utah Poetry Society, Junior Creative Writing Program, and Utah State Poet of the Year contest—through which she published 18 volumes of community poetry.

But this book isn't about Kathryn Kay's community work; it's about her contributions to the craft she loved so much and a collection of previously published works along with writings from her "retirement."

It would tickle my grandma to no end to think that her words might touch a generation living in a completely different century than her. And she would absolutely glow to imagine she might inspire new writers to find the words within themselves to express the heartfelt emotions that connect us all.

In addition, I include some of Kathryn's writing notes at the end of this book that may seem random, but they will not let me sleep unless I include them in the publication. And I like sleep, so they're included.

All in all, this book has five sections.

The first section includes poems from Kathryn Kay's three published books. Not *all* of the poems from those publications are included here, but enough to give you a stroll through a world seen through her eyes.

Section 2 is a collection of poems that never made it past random scraps of paper and yellow notepads during her lifetime.

Each of these poems is being published here for the first time.

Section 3 includes a few of the proverbs and more spiritual thoughts my grandma had while raising her children. Sections 4 & 5 include tips on public speaking and writing haiku, respectively.

My hope is that her words will help you connect to your inner-self and those around you in a way that revitalizes you.

Words have the power to do that, and my grandma had the gift of getting words to say exactly what she wanted them to say.

May they work their magic in your life and brighten your path.

NOTE: Kathryn's years in Hollywood taught her Taylor Swift's lesson about owning your own catalog long before Taylor was born. Kathryn Kay firmly believed in always keeping your copyright and renewing it when it's about to lapse, in case future generations can use it.

This means, by her own hand, all of Kathryn's published work is still in copyright and not to be used without written permission from her son.

So, please, respect the wishes of the 90-pound woman who lived the best life she knew how while making sure no one owned her or her work by the time she was done.

Also, know that Kathryn advises you to take similar pride in your own work and suggests you protect it just as fervently.

About the Illustrations

All of the illustrations on the cover are by an artist named Plot. We don't know much about Plot outside of the fact that he or she was my grandma's favorite illustrator and Plot's sketches are almost synonymous with a book of Kathryn Kay poems.

If you know who Plot is and where to find more of their work, give me a shout @SheralynPratt on either Twitter or Instagram.

In the meantime, I hope you enjoy Plot's signature style from a bygone era.

Table of Contents

Classic Kay

Poems in this section are selections from Kathryn Kay's
published works:

With Tongue in Cheek and Heart on Sleeve

If the Shoe Fits

Practically Apparent

POSSIBLE SQUEEZE PLAY

This advice I
chanced upon
that's influenced me quite a lot—
"IF THE SHOE FITS—put it on!"
Just look what Cinderella got!

GOD'S IN A THIMBLE

God's in a thimble
as small as a dot
or ten times as large as the sea.
He's mostly in heaven, but
sometimes He's not,
'cause sometimes He's right here in me!

ARMOUR

        I ask for one
        thing only,
one moment bathed in
understanding's light,
then, tho my path be lonely,
I shall not fear the night.

PROBLEM

They tell me only God
can make a tree
and that He watches every sparrow's flight
and yet it seems I have enough in me
alone, to keep Him busy day and night.

DEPRESSING CONVICTION

        I think
        that what I want
mostly to do
is to talk simply
but I am afraid
that what
I do mostly
is simply
talk.

GOD KNOWS

        God knows the language
        that I speak,
His eyes can see thru any pose,
and if my tongue is in my cheek
or not, God knows.

LITTLE PEOPLE

When folk try to impress me
they're important,
I smile a bit at their absurd pomposity.
God, let such aims in me be self-abortant,
don't let me ever take myself too seriously!

REMEDIAL

If only I could write
the way I feel—
with all the fire that fills my lonely state—
perhaps, then all my writing would be real—
could every pore become articulate.
And yet the way I feel is wrong, or so
"they" tell me, guessing passion I conceal.
That's why I'm forced to write like this and know
that only you can right the way I feel.

ANENT NEGLECT

Young as the evening,
but all alone—
this picture lacks a certain touch.
You see that quiet telephone?
I'm hot—but I'm not bothered much!

CAREERIST

And I can smile
at futile sorrow,
I who am too wise for tears,
I for whom no vague tomorrow
holds retributory fears;
and I make brilliant conversation,
speak of love in level tone;
but what a silly occupation—
talking in your sleep, alone!

GREGARIAN

Waiting for a man
outside a door
of any kind,
or in a car,
waiting for a man
an hour or more
time unconfined
beneath a star,
waiting for a man
outside a store
I shouldn't mind
it, insofar,
as it's this certain man
I'm waiting for,
I've lived to find
that most girls are
waiting for a man!

THE ANT'S DECISION

While I'm still young
I'm going to steal
some memories of living,
to have when I'm too old to feel
the ecstasies of giving.

SUCKER'S SOLILOQUY

How contradictory
life's been
to me, how round about...
Somehow, I'm always taken in
each time I'm taken out.

CATALINA

Like the mainland,
you, my sweet,
are large and competently get things done—
comparatively, I'm petite—
but colorful—and lots more fun!

TO AN IMPETUOUS LOVER

Be patient,
oh, my dearest,
when I shrink back from your touch,
it's only from the sheerest
joy, because it means so much
to me to think you care,
I cannot love you lightly
in just a casual affair—
remember, just tonight, we
chanced upon each other's hearts.
Don't wonder that I doubt you,
who are so skilled in lover's arts—
I could be mad about you;
but, tho I long to kiss you, sweet,
and feel your strong arms crush me—
if you would make the thrill complete—
my darling—never rush me!!

HOSPITALIZATION

I used to be so sane
and cool and calm,
at least, that's how I like to think I was,
before love tossed my dormant heart a bomb
and wrapped my reason in shining gauze
which quite befogs me in a roseate cloud
of dreams come true. Now, suddenly I find
the various talents with which I'm endowed
clogged up and helpless in my febrile mind.
My thoughts are all at sea. I stultify
in happiness I've never known before.
Perhaps that's why I dread the day that I
perforce revert to normalcy once more.

DUBIOUS CONSOLATION

      I've eaten my words
      and I've swallowed my pride
and I find it a difficult diet.
Each meal leaves me feeling more hollow inside
with a very disturbing unquiet.
It isn't the fare I thot love would choose
to exercise my epiglottis
but being so starved who am I to refuse?
At least I've learned what food for thot is.

IT IS TO LAUGH

It is to laugh
that we were given senses
of humor, there our only power lies.
This one small gift is all that recompenses
a man for seeing life thru human eyes.
It is to hope that we have hearts, thus letting
our minds be free to separate life's chaff
to serve its purpose, and keep us from forgetting
what really glorious fun it is to laugh.

PURE IN HEART

My faith in you
is as a thing apart
from all the tumult in a world of flux
and vacillation, where love reconstructs
and readjusts itself at will. My heart,
in spite of all the pressure brought to bear
upon it, somehow, never stoops to doubt.
It stands immutable, while all about
is turbulence, and even when despair
seeps in, as it is wont to do at times,
and hope hangs low, its faith remains secure.
My head, however, is not quite so sure
and rears its skeptic self throughout my rhymes.

CONDITIONED

It's not that
I don't love you,
I hate to be the chaser—
when one is born a pencil
one can't be an eraser!

SONG OF THE TIMID SOULS

We are not
the darers, are we?
And to take a chance we're loath.
It's better to be safe than sorry....
but it's the devil when you're both!

GOLDFISH PRIVACY

Oh, other poets write
about the daffodils in spring,
the flitting of a butterfly at play;
the babbling of a brook,
the way the little birdies sing,
and sundry other things which sound so gay;
and they can hide their tears and
put their hearts upon the shelf
to sing for hours of some capricious caper.
But, no! I can't do that! I have to crucify myself
for all the world to see it there on paper!

FOUNDATIONS

Why can't I live
life daily
nor delve into the past,
why can't I take love gaily
nor long for it to last?
As long as we're together
and happy to be here,
why must I worry whether
regrets will come next year?
For some silly future sorrow
I refuse this hour's delight—
must I always build tomorrow
on the way I feel tonight?

MODERN METHOD

Where's the cooperation
of that old time fire brigade
that used to pass the buckets all along the line?
From much abbreviation now folks figure,
I'm afraid, if they can simply pass the buck,
they're doing fine.

THE MORE FOOL I

It's not as tho
I were a simple maiden;
I know the ways of life and love and men,
how quickly joyous hearts are heavy laden,
how quickly hopes that rise can fall again.
It's not as tho I hadn't touched the fire.
I know how easily one's fingers burn,
I know the anticlimax of desire,
these things and many more I had to learn.
And yet, if love once more should come to seek
me,
I'd probably fling open wide, my door,
and give my heart and soul to him completely,
forgetting all I ever learned before.

SIMILE

           You're like the rose
           that stands apart,
    secure within its own conceit,
    and flow'rs of lesser fragrance scorns—
    but I could find it in my heart
    to wish you weren't quite so sweet
    and had a few less thorns.

CATALOGUED

    Tho we'd like to think
    our love is everlasting
and pretend it will grow deeper year by year,
it's impossible to change our fate's forecasting—
this is really just a passion fancy, dear.

FEMALE OF THE SPECIES

And you can leave me
callously
and never try to see my face again?
Oh, God, how very diff'rently
You made women love than men!

ROUTINE

Another year,
another love,
two more clear-cut eyes;
another tear
and up above,
the moon, and stars, and skies;
another week
a softer cheek,
and lips to trace it tenderly;
another kiss,
and after this,
another memory.

GENTLEMEN

Oh, this is the tale
of the too gentle men,
their appeal was, I fear, mostly mental.
Unfortunately they were too gentle men,
entirely too, too gentle.

APPLIED PSYCHOLOGY

You said our love
would never last.
My love that fact denied.
But now I guess our love is past.
I hope you're satisfied!

BRAVADO

I don't care
if you desert me,
I've had other loves before,
one more parting will not hurt me,
there will probably be more.
I don't mind if you forget me,
I've forgotten lots of men,
I'll forget you if you'll let me,
life will be more simple, then.
What if I mean nothing to you,
that won't break my heart you know—
Lord! You don't believe me, do you?
Please, dear God, don't let him go!!

ON SECOND THOUGHT

Don't ever let me know
that I can hurt you
but rather, let me think you wouldn't care
so very much if ever I desert you,
or prove to be unworthy or unfair.
Don't let me see your need, for it might blind
me
to what I really feel, and in a way,
I am afraid I'd let that knowledge bind me,
for fear of hurting you, perhaps I'd stay.
My love must not be influenced by knowing
how desperately you depend on me.
I must not stay because I know my going
would cause you pain. My love needs must
be free.
And yet, if you should do as I'm suggesting,
pretend indiff'rence should I stray afar,
I know I'd be the first to stop protesting . . .
Perhaps we'd better leave things as they
are.

THOUGHT AT THANKSGIVING

Sweet words and smiles
were quite the least
life used to fatten up my heart—
I didn't know that at love's feast
it was to play the turkey's part.

LONG STORY

It takes so many
paragraphs
to tell why God invented laughs.

INCENDIARY

You lit the flame
which feeds desire
but you are not a good Boy Scout,
for Boy Scouts never leave a fire
until they've put the damn thing out!

PLASTICITY

Oh, do not fear
for me, my friend,
and pity not my ache,
because you see, my heart may bend
but it will never break!

ATHLETIC MINDED

"Mental bruises
and contusions"
reads my medical report,
"caused from jumping to conclusions
and falling short."

TWICE SHY

My faith and my trust
were the knives that you used,
my dreams were the things that you tore—
but now that it's over and love has excused,
dare I give you the weapons once more?

COMPARISON

Do not think me
too callous
when my sorrow doesn't linger—
when one has lost an arm
one doesn't cry to lose a finger.

LESSON

My sorrow now
is many-mooned
but I have lived to learn
that altho time can heal a wound
old scars can ache and burn.

MASOCHISM

Instead of
trying to forget
why do I treasure everything
that brings me, in an icy sweat,
the torture of remembering?

PRE-REVOLT

Too long have I been housed
with weary things.
I must get out and gaze up at the sky
where winds are brave and free and somehow, I
must emulate the city sparrows' wings
which, with a few defiant fluttering,
can take birds up to fresh blue that is high
above the squalor of the streets. God, I must try
to feel the courage that a shaft of sunlight brings
to warm a waiting world and make it bright.
This cloistered way I live is all so wrong.
I must remember how it feels to fight
for my beliefs, to struggle and be strong.
I need a new perspective, one that's right—
I have been housed with weary things too long!

PLEA FOR CONTENTMENT

And pray, let not
my deeds be touched
by an absurd regret—
teach me not to expect too much
nor be dissatisfied with what I get.

SOMEWHAT PARADOXICAL SITUATION

God, he sits by my side
and holds my hand,
he, who has been so long away.
I look at him, trying to understand
and wait for the words he does not say.
God, why is it we are the way we are?
Why is his silence so verbose?
It's only when he is near, he's far,
when he's away, we're awf'ly close!

TO A WISTFUL GOD

I'll bet You have
Your wistful moments, God,
You cannot always be pleased with Your plans.
When You make things as intricate as man's
desires, You can't sit back and just applaud
Yourself forever, for a job well done.
You complicate his body with a soul
and when one has the other in control
the conflict isn't pretty, God, nor one
of which You could be proud or want to boast.
You have Your disappointments, too, I guess,
with all the silly people You must bless;
You give a man the things he wants the most
and find that he is still dissatisfied.
I do not mind because You wish an act
of Yours might go right just for once. In fact,
I'm glad that You're not smug and filled with pride.
It brings me, somehow, much closer to You,
You see, I have my wistful moments, too.

LET ME BE WORTHY

Please God, help me to help the ones
who look to me for aid,
let me think clearly at the time when they're
confused.
Help me to know what's right, nor let me be afraid
the trust they place in me will ever be abused.
Let me feel sure within myself that I am strong
with the unfailing strength that true conviction
gives.
If need be let my knowledge carry them along
until the time they realize theirs also lives.
Let me have confidence in my ability
to guide them. Never let me doubt the words I say,
and everything they think I am, please, let me be,
help me to never fail them, God, in any way.
Let me be wise that I may pass such wisdom on
to those whose destinies You've placed within my
hands.
God, from my judgment let all prejudice be gone,
give me instead the tolerance this life demands.
They look to me for help and I must never let them
know
how much I'm frightened at my vast responsibility,
I'll do my best, I'll help them every way I can, but so
that I may be more worthy of their faith, please
God, help me.

ONE SHEEP

        God, I don't know how to start
        or what to say.
I do not know the language of a formal prayer
so long it's been since my heart felt the urge to
pray,
so long I've made believe no need to pray was
there.
But, God, somehow I don't believe You are the kind
to hold a grudge for what I have or haven't done,
and if I just start praying I know You won't mind
or worry much about the way my prayer's begun.
It's over. I've been wrong and I'm not going to
make
a lot of fancy promises that may not last,
a lot of crazy vows I'm weak enough to break.
You see, I have discovered mem'ries can be short,
and even tho right now my feet are on the ground,
it's hard to keep them there, so much comes to
distort
my sense of values and to twist my views around.
I don't know yet if I can find the way to You,
I am afraid I'm apt to falter now and then,
but I will do the most that anyone can do,
if You'll have patience, honest, God, I'll try! Amen.

FIRST AID

The fact I might smile
later on
doesn't cheer me much, somehow—
don't stall me with some vague "anon,"
I need a laugh right now!

PRACTICAL CERTAINTY

If I were only
    sweet sixteen
and hadn't seen the things I've seen
and hadn't done the things I've done
I'll bet you I'd be having fun!

CHRISTMAS KNIGHT

You're just like
Santa Claus, my dear,
I see you only once a year—
you bring your pack of tales, unmatched
in wonder, with no strings attached.
You speak of love that's deep, eternal—
and once more I know flutters vernal—
But also, just like Santa Claus
there is no you, nor ever was,
your love is just a cozy myth—
I like to flatter myself with
the while I use with rueful laughter
the perfume I have named you after.

DEPARTURE

You opened the doors
of your heart and taught
me the art of a game called "Supposing"—
Ah, doors are most wonderful things, I thought.
You see—for a moment I almost forgot
that doors have a habit—of closing.

YOU'VE MADE ME OLD

You've made me old,
for now I see
how very young I used to be—
the things that I believed were true
the things I said—and thought I knew.
You've made me wise, for now I know
of this and that and so and so.
You've made me sad, for you reveal
the way I used to think and feel,
and you have made me realize
perhaps I'm older than I'm wise—
perhaps there are degrees in age—
I've passed the kindergarten stage—
but may God bless the man—or men
who makes me feel quite young again!

THREAT

Another
night
without you
may turn
into
another
night
without you.

BONDAGE

 And I shall not be free
 by simply leaving
the things I love in you. I can't pretend
that by a swift departure I can end
these countless hours I spend in self-deceiving
nor stop this senseless habit of believing,
of hoping some day splintered hearts will mend.
No, when I go I know I'll but append
another chapter to my book of grieving.
And not until I cease to think about you,
or hear your name and quite diff'rent be,
or mention various times I used to doubt you
as simple conversation, casually;
'til I have learned at night to dream without you
'til then, but not 'til then shall I be free!

WHISTLE IN THE DARK

How will I fill my time
away from you
who fill my pulsing body, heart and mind?
What can I ever find for me to do?
What is there that is left for me to find?
Such was my frightened cry when first you left,
for then I could not think of anything
except that with you gone I'd be bereft
of all the things I knew our love could bring.
Together we had found so very much
of loveliness, I knew none could remain,
and every single memory I'd clutch
I thought would ultimately bring me pain
for that it could not be renewed.
That is not true. So fully did we live
each moment of our fleeting interlude
that we know life has nothing more to give;
no joy more poignant than joy we have known,
no star more brilliant than stars we have seen,
too close we've been to ever be alone
again. We've learned all life can mean.
That knowledge is a white torch shining clear
to light the way I go, triumphantly.
How fill my time away from you? My dear,
there isn't any such—nor can there be!

CONSTRUCTIVE CRITICISM

Of course, it's not for me
to criticize
the way that You have planned it—
You're the Boss and what You say must go.
Sure! Break my heart, but why not make me wise
enough to understand it?
It's this awful wond'ring that hurts me so!

DIFFICULT CREED

If only I could live
from day to day,
nor think of what is past, nor what's to be,
that is my only prayer, my only plea;
I do not beg to be forever gay,
for flowers to be strewn along my way,
but only for the courage to be free
of small regrets, of hope's stupidity,
and to accept the present. This I pray:
Give me this day my daily bread, no more.
Just let me live each moment 'til it dies,
and should life offer love, let me adore
for one brief instant, asking for no ties
to join the future to what's gone before,
and tho I seem a fool, I shall be wise.

PROTECTION

I smile at the sweet things
you say to me
but don't you realize,
the reason I smile is so you won't see
the tears behind my eyes?

AFTERMATH

Now that it's through
I can laugh at my fears,
my aches and my bruises and scars—
what if my eyes are all snarled up with
tears—my thoughts are a tangle of stars!

ESTABLISHED FACT

On mountain tops or by the sea,
in cities or on farms,
a man can easily find sanctuary;
but woman isn't safe until she's in her husband's
arms,
and even then, she isn't very.

A VERY SAD REFLECTION

In a little while
you will forget my ways;
the sudden way I smile,
the way I twist a phrase;
the simple things it takes
for me to be content,
and everything that makes
me different.
You laugh now at my threat,
and make me swift denial,
but I know you'll forget
in a little while.

PRAYER IN A DIVORCE COURT

God, these folk who tied knots
at the marriage altar
seem prone to overlook its fundamental use,
to many it's a slip-knot, while to some a halter,
and God, I greatly fear to some it is a noose.
Please God, if in the future I should find love's
unction,
help me to tie the marriage knot again some day,
to serve not a perverted, but its truest function,
tying two loose ends together so they'll stay!

WITHOUT FANFARE

I always knew
that someday you'd appear
and waited patiently,
but, I hardly knew that you were here,
you came so quietly!

LITTLE LADDERS

I know, now
that I have you near,
the love affairs that I once knew,
were simply little ladders, dear,
that I was climbing up to you!

EDUCATION

Now, there'll be
no other love for me
except the love you make—
I was satisfied with bread, you see,
until I tasted cake!

DECISION

If there
is some thing
we can't share
then there
is something
we can't share.

LAST MARRIAGE

I'd like to make this
my last marriage, God,
I want to make it permanent and fast,
I do not mean like my last marriage, God,
that is completely over with and past,
but please, please make this my last
marriage, God,
I mean, God, make it last!

EXAMINING BOARD

The better
to confirm suspicion
I hie off to our physician,
like guinea pig in unfamiliar scene,
and, as I take the weird position
assumed by gals in my condition,
remind myself that this is pure routine.
Modestly, in white sheet, covered
by a nurse who, bland has hovered,
I lie supine with limbs flared to the skies;
sporadic bits of conversation
augment the investigation
as doctor probes and pokes and verifies.
Tho I assure you I'm no prudist,
neither is my cult a nudist,
and tho I know it's all matter of course,
I can't pretend I'm not a-spraddle
with feet in stirrups but no saddle
and nothing where there ought to be a
horse!

NEWTON NOTWITHSTANDING

I sit me down
with small anticipation
no more do I revel when I sup;
it offers me but little consolation
when to my lips I place a steaming cup,
since you've reversed the law of gravitation
and what goes down now, thanks to you,
comes up!

NO SISSY THIS

What if it's not a boy?
Well, sue me!
I call him Spud or Butch or Spike
because he is doing to me
I find most unladylike!

SUCCESS!

Says Hollywood,
"You must put on a big front
if you would reach fame's highest pinnacle."
To me that seemed just a publicity stunt
and the thot made me, quite frankly, cynical;
but nature, the wag, put the trick in her bag
and she said, "Let's abide by the ruling."
Now I must confess, as I struggle to dress,
I've put on a big front and no fooling!

FANCY

    I gaze in unfeigned
    fascination
at where I've put on pounds and ounces,
like Buddha, lost in contemplation,
except that what I'm watching, bounces!

BEATEN PATH

I find there's one thing
in this set-up
that somehow seems to make me get up
a lot more often than I ever used to.
Tho my exaggerated plumbing
is due, no doubt, to baby's coming
I must retreat more than, off-hand, I'd choose to.
With every well directed thump
ups-a-daisy, I must jump,
day or night there seems to be no lenience;
and thanks to these activities
I've got a path worn to my knees
from me to our home's handiest convenience!

CONVERSATION AT DAWN

Here now, baby,
stop that kicking,
are you partly kangaroo?
That's my tender side you're sticking,
I don't do like that to you!
Just because my form you're rounding
you don't have to thrash about,
here now, baby, stop that pounding,
mother knows that you want out.
Listen, I've some things to tell you
ere you greet the light of day.
Down the river life will sell you,
hear what mother has to say.
Might as well stop all that knocking,
life's not yours to beck and call,
quiet, darling, mother's talking,
life's a humpty-dumpty wall.
You'd leave your present safety, maybe,
for measles, mumps and whooping cough?
Lie quiet and stop kicking, baby,
you don't know when you're well off!

SONG AT SEVEN MONTHS

Of course I feel you
poke and nudge,
but why rush headlong into strife?
Child, just remember nature's judge
has sentenced you nine months to life.
From quarters close and far from starry
I know you'd dearly love to climb,
but, believe me, babe, we'd both be sorry
if you got out before your time!

THE LOW-DOWN

                    Keep on with your hops
                    and skipping,
          carry on your merry pace,
          but you must admit you're slipping,
          time will put you in your place.
          Thump around in high elation,
          little inner gadabout,
          I have inside information
          you will soon be down and out!

FIGURATIVELY

I gaze at glamour
gals in ads
with silhouettes, all lithe and lissom,
flanked by fascinated lads
who obviously ache to kiss 'em.
But small the good for me to mope
about the slender lines I covet,
while I look like a mountain slope,
grand, of course, but hard to love it.
So I won't rue my bulging belt
which covers poundage more than thirty;
let them have their figures svelte
as long as you still think I'm purty!

OVER-DUEING IT

Something is completely
out of line—
I'm sure that I have kept track right along—
one, two, three, four, five, six, seven, eight, nine—
I wonder if I could have counted wrong?

AT TOO LONG LAST

Guess you think
you're mighty clever,
all these nine months I've been waiting;
but this can't go on forever,
better stop procrastinating.
Think how badly you have used me,
smug because I can't get at you,
kicked and otherwise abused me,
come on out, you scaredy-cat, you!

NO SIGN YET

If I thot you
believed in signs
I'd get me some to hang about
down there within the deep confines
of me, marked "Exit—this way out!"

WELCOME

Get prepared, child
take your pose,
clench your fists and bend them double,
take it from someone who knows,
you're coming headfirst into trouble!

MOTHER'S DAY

Five days God worked
to make this world
the very best that He'd created—
and then He sat with brow all furled,
the whole thing seemed so complicated.
"I'll have to have some help, somehow,
in passing on this life to others"—
The answer came. He smoothed His brow
and on the sixth day He made mothers,
and babies were. And life went on—
maternity was deep invested
in woman's heart—God's cares were gone—
and on the seventh day He rested.

TO A YOUNG A MOTHER

        I cannot realize
        that you have undergone
the oldest duplication known on earth.
You seem so very young to have been let in on
the secrets of the wonder we call birth,
and altho I reiterate the fact so bland
I cannot make myself believe nor
understand that it is true.
You seem so young to be so old
to know so much—
you know thru you, another life's begun.
You know against your breast
your baby's pulsing touch,
that you are two who but so recently were one.
I can't believe it, tho I know that it is so,
and when you gaze down on that tiny head, I
know no more can you.

WHAT ARE YOU THINKING?

　　　　Listen, God, listen to the world
　　　　that You created,
just listen, God, to what is happening down here!
Hear the agony-filled cries of men nobody hated,
of men who die for reasons never wholly clear.
Can You hear the wild cacophony that bombs are
making
in their death-strewing life, so violently brief?
You, Who can hear the sob a heart makes when
it's breaking,
what must You hear in this accumulated grief?
Listen, can You hear the awful quiet of no
laughter,
the poignant stillness of the gayest sound on
earth?
Can You hear the trembling of a child's lips after
he's learned to know the feeling of fear-stifled
mirth?
Skies once peaceful now are loud with deadly
man-made thunder,
hope's gallant song is silenced by greed's firing-
squad.
Can You hear this bedlam in Your world? If so, I
wonder,
what are You thinking as You listen, God?

WE IN THE DARK

I guess You know
what You are doing, God,
it's only folk like me who get confused.
It's too much to expect a little clod
of human stuff to know the methods used
in handling worlds. It must suffice for me
to carefully remind myself that You
must have Your reasons, reasons I can't see
for doing the heart-wrenching things You do.
I try to quell my fears with this belief
for I could never hope to understand
a reason that would justify the grief
that Your idea of life seems to demand,
nor am I yet presumptuous enough
to think I could expect You to explain
Your deeds to me. In this mad Blind Man's Bluff
called living, it seems that I must remain
the one whirled in the dark, while You stand by
to guide my stumbling.

God, I'm not to blame
if sometimes I can't help but wonder why
You put so many horrors in the game.
To me it's a bewild'ring sort of world
where nothing seems to make sense any more.
You teach us to love peace and then we're hurled
into the gross stupidity of war.
It isn't that I ever want to doubt
the wisdom of Your ways. I trust in You,
but there's so much I cannot figure out,
not having an omniscient point of view.
We see this world of Yours from two extremes,
from where You are it's plain as A B C,
but God, please don't forget the way it seems
to little fellows in the dark, like me.

TO ME

And there shall be no need
to comfort thee
who understood her most and loved her best.
You know her heart, tho' stilled within her breast
will pulse and throb throughout eternity
in lovely things. 'Tis God's consistency.
There is no death, there's only constant change.
When night turns into day—'tis not so strange,
and night, for her, has dawned to brilliancy.
One does not mourn to see a butterfly
emerge with splendor from an old cocoon,
nor weep when spring ends wintertime nor sigh
at ever-varying stages of the moon.
In ev'ry gentle breeze you'll feel her breath
and you'll look up and smile . . . There is no death!

TO JO

You cannot tell
what happiness or sorrow lies in wait
behind the screen of hours yet to be.
Nobody knows. We can't anticipate
tomorrow's sun, nor its apostrophe.
There was no way for us to look ahead
and see that you so quickly were to go;
there are so many things you would have said,
so many things you'd like to have me know.
How could we guess that you'd so soon be gone,
without a chance to even say goodby,
that all the lovely things we had planned on
so confidently were so soon to die.
And you who love to help so very much
would never leave me thus. I know you long
to give to me some reassuring touch
to show the way; to teach me to be strong.
I ache to understand the why and how,
so, knowing, as I do, your thoughts so well,
the hardest part for you must be that now
you know the answers for me and
you cannot tell.

THIS DARKNESS, TOO

God, how do I go on from here?
What happens, now?
The only world I care about is gone.
I know I must go on some way but how, God,
how?
There seems so little left to build upon.
The fine incentives that I had before are dead,
and what did all my eager effort prove?
Futility, perhaps, but God, what lies ahead?
What is the next move when there is no move?
I know I'm not the only one who feels like this,
the world itself is torn and troubled, too.
It waits the time when doubt will find its nemesis
as night in day, as...oh, God, is that the clue?
The answer?...God, I think I see now why You gave
the promise of a dawn to every night....
God, suddenly it is no effort to be brave—
this darkness, too, will pass into the light!

WHAT CAN I GIVE

What can I give
to a little boy
I love in the way I love you,
something the future cannot destroy
or change in the way futures do?
What can I give to two tiny hands
that already cuddle my heart?
Yours are such simple, so few demands,
small boy, with your dreams at their start.
Beads that can dazzle and make a noise
and you're satisfied for the nonce,
but—life gets harder for little boys
and starts complicating their wants.
Where can I find a gift I can give
to help when the going gets rough?
I can give you my life for as long as I live
oh, but that's not enough—not enough!

FIRST VALENTINE

I wonder,
little baby boy,
what valentines life has in store
to drop beside your waiting door—
will they bring grief or joy?
And if it's grief, will you be strong
and keep that little head on high,
nor ever let those wide eyes cry,
for that life's jumbled up and wrong?
Oh, little boy, so fresh and fine
with all your days so shiny new,
what valentines are there for you?
Please God, send them from love like mine!

LAST MESSAGE

Know this, then, when time comes
I must leave you
with that intangible, a memory,
let there be nothing in such thought to grieve you.
Death proves life's indestructibility.
We know that physically all things must perish.
Man cannot cling to loved things that are his
and we but build up heartache when we cherish.
The more we love, the harder parting is,
but if your heart begins to feel tears starting,
remind it if it's missing me some night
that our is just a temporary parting.
I'm only waiting for you out of sight.

Unpublished Poems

… found on paper scraps &
yellow notepads

Note: These poems are formatted as she wrote them
(without with her signature two-line indent) and are
presented in "found" order. If she noted the dated she wrote
it, that is also included.

KEEPING MY DISTANCE

I'm making a bunch of twelve-foot poles
for I intend to give them when they're done
to all those learned doctors, bless their souls,
who will not touch me with a ten-foot one.

—1982, '83, '84, '84, '86, '87, '88, '89, '90,
ad infinitum

ABOUT: GRAVE TURNING

The world has this fierce propensity
to shock and violently misbehave.
It's clear my future's main activity
will be a whirling dervish in my grave.

—April 9, 2001 (age 94)

NO HURT FEELINGS

The angry words you spoke to me
when you were so upset
should not disturb you;
actually, I have not heard them yet.
For love, anticipating tears,
taught me the useful art
to never listen with my ears
but only with my heart.

—September 11, 1998 (age 91)

MY HANG-UP

I'd like to emulate the bee
whose engine makes him buzz,
for I admire his industry
and everything he does.
I really want to do my part
and valiantly I try—
it's only that I know
I'm just a butterfly.

—1971

SO IMPERCEPTIBLE THE CHANGE

So imperceptible the change of seed
to bud to blossom, then fading;
we are unaware of each state to the next.
We never knew till it was through.
We see only the results, not the happening.

Somehow, in the same strange way,
the blend and shading of youth to age
is one which can compare in imperceptibility.
When does youth end, old age begin?

It is so strange—so imperceptible the changes.
Unobserved by me, my once-smooth skin
has not been seared by too many August suns.
Now, autumn parchments my shriveling cheek,
which sags here and there,
over an unnoticed long-while.

But I feel myself smile,
for, although December snow is whitening my hair,
one thought consoles me as I realize
my memory sparkles with Fourth of Julys.
And April is still in my eyes,
even though, imperceptibly,
age is having its way with me.

—Year Unknown

ORIGIN OF MURPHY'S LAW

I lack the words with which to curse
but I knew them, I'd be glad to;
I think, at last, I've had the worse
I've always heard thing go from "bad" to.

—Year Unknown

PERFECT BIRTHDAY CARD

Altho I have tried very hard
to find a really clever card,
somehow, when all was said and done
I couldn't find a single one
that said just what I wanted it to say
and so I said, "Oh, what the heck,
I'll just send you a birthday check—I
think you'd rather have that anyway."

—Year Unknown

FETTLED DEBT

Nothing will put you
in a fine fettle
as much as getting
out of debt'll.

—Year Unknown

DEAD END

> I have found this face is true:
> worry's like a rocking chair
> it serves as something you can do
> but it won't get you anywhere.

> —Year Unknown

MAKING BRIGHT SIDES

I don't indulge in puerile whining
I leave that to the weaker crowds—
the while I hemstitch silver linings
on the all the insides of my clouds.

—Dec 22, 1982

WORRY, WORRY

I thought love was supposed to sooth
but, brother, was I wrong!
For now I know my life was smooth
until you came along.
Whatever was I thinking of?
How come I felt no qualm?
Hello, longing; enter, love,
goodbye peace and calm.

—Year Unknown

STYMIED

When I was young I'd grab my pen
and graphically describe it when
my heart would break or become smitten
but now I'm in a sorry plight
because the things I want to write,
unfortunately, I've already written.

—Year Unknown

RULE FOR PROCRASTINATORS

If you must wait till the right time to do it,
you'll find life somehow prevents you,
in some way, from getting to it.
A single truth we cannot disavow:
the only right time is right now.

—Year Unknown

NO TITLE

Avert your eyes when you look at me
—know that age is to blame.
Remember me as I used to be
and not this caricature I became.

- September 22, 2000

GOOD MORNING

I gather my body to greet the day
and adapt myself to the weather.
I gather my body
for it is the way
I hold all my pains together.

—September 20, 2000

TO MY FATHER

I don't need a calendar day set apart
to tell you how deeply I care,
for there is so very much in my heart
you can't help but know is there.
The older I grow,
I am more positive you're the finest man I ever
knew.
My heart is more grateful each moment I live
that I have a father like you!

—Year Unknown

GOING, GOING, GUNG

My energy is running low,
I fear my spring has sprung.
I still have little spurts of "Ho"
but where, oh where's, my "Gung"?

—1987

THIS MOMENT, NOW

This moment is eternity.
Eternity is now.
It has no end,
no beginning.
Like intelligence,
it always was, is,
and will be.
It will not change,
never be different
from what it is now.
Things change,
people change,
worlds change,
but eternity remains constant.
Time is a metronome,
a device which enables man
to measure his heartbeats.
Time is man's method
of counting inexorable always-ness,
the ever-ness of eternity
which we can know in this moment
of now.

—1972

NECESSITY DICTATES

There'll be times you'll have to rearrange
your life into a different space,
when you face that fact that you can change
when you can't change the facts you face.

—Year Unknown

NO MERE SKELETONS

With effort, I remember when
girls were girls and men were men
and sex was something we had no doubt of
and closets, as they should have been,
were places to hang up clothes in,
not just somewhere for someone to come out of.

—1981

NOT DEEP ENOUGH

I am a youth who is far from callow,
if I seem harsh I shall explain:
I fell in love; the girl was shallow
and I stubbed my widdle bwain.

—Year Unknown

GETTING NO PLACE

There's one thing I would like to know
—for it would help me if I knew—
where is the place they call "and fro"
I'm always running to?

—February 1, 1990

IN RETROSPECT

I contemplate the life I've led,
I never sat upon the fence.
When faced with tears,
I laughed instead.
And that, as Mr. Frost has said,
made all the difference.

—May 1, 1989

RE: BACKS AND BURDENS

Unfortunately, I don't have a brain
that's smart enough to make me understand
why I'm so thrown off balance, or explain
why life gets so completely out of hand.
The Lord says burdens we are made to bear
are fitted to each individual back.
There's no way to successfully compare
the heaviness of loads we have to pack.
And , so if I deserve this kind of burden,
that is, considering its heft and size,
I think perhaps I can be fairly certain
I must be very special in his eyes.
It's very complimentary, if true—
he thinks my back is stronger than I do.

—Year Unknown

A PARENT SPEAKS

My child, how can I express the happiness I feel
because you are the kind of child you are.
Each time I look at you,
I struggle to conceal my tears of pride,
altho I've managed to thus far.
You see, my joy is not just happiness alone;
it's mixed with pride that what you are
was given to me to be my child,
for me to guide and call my own,
and with gratitude because God let this come to
be.
You fulfill all the hopes and dreams I ever had
by simply being you,
an entity apart which, by some miracle, is mine.
I'm glad you're not aware of this commotion in my
heart,
for I must not encumber you with too much love.
My child, I only want your heart to understand.
Tho love is something we cannot have too much of,
it must be glimpsed within my eyes, touched thru my
hand.
Had you been different, I guess I've have loved you
,too,
but I love you, not just because you're mine,
but that you're you,
the same way God loves you because you're His!

—Year Unknown

SUFFICIENT GLORY

You owe me nothing
just because I gave you birth.
I don't concur with all this talk of obligation.
The fact I was the door thru which you entered
earth
does not per se apportion me consideration.
You didn't ask to come—at least that I know of;
that I gave you a certain form is incidental.
I'm not entitled to a special kind of love.
The part God let me play was wholly instrumental
to give your soul a tangibility.
You owe your gift of life to Him, not me...
Of course, if, after you're completely on your own,
you choose to love me deeply,
that's all to the good;
but love me as a person, for myself alone,
and not because you are my child and feel you
should.
Let us be factual, if we can, in our relation.
As mother, I am but a line from which you swerve.
My having been allowed to share in your creation
gives me a touch of Godness I can never quite
deserve.
If you love me, my child, so much the better,
but it is I, not you, who am the debtor.

—Year Unknown

NOR CALL ME NOBLE

You make me sound so noble
when you speak of what I do,
as though I should be proud
of simply doing good.
You say that I am different from the rest
because you think I do more than I should.
There is no reason I should unique
or labeled a do-gooder.
Is there a limit to a blue sky or a cloud,
or to the times one turns another cheek,
a limit to how much good one should do?
You say I am so different from the norm.
Who sets the norm? Who determines
how much time one would spend to help a friend?
Your reasoning, to me, seems somewhat absurd.
Since when has altruism become a dirty word?
Do good to one another is a creed
advanced in unadorned simplicity.
And so I help someone in temporary need.
It is a way of life that pleases me.

—Year Unknown

SMALL VICTORY

They say hang on
when it is tough going,
that this will always win out in the end.
But maybe that's their martyr complex showing.
At any rate, it's hard to comprehend.
For, sometimes, it's more the wise to be a quitter,
it is a way of facing a mistake.
To know discouragement and not be bitter
is a decision that is always hard to make.
There is a time for firm determination
but there can be exceptions to each law.
Rather than admit wrong calculation
it can be easier to stay than to withdraw.
Sometimes, I wish the ones with all their learning
would remember there are other ways to win.
Sometimes, the only victory worth earning
is the one achieved by simply giving in.

—Year Unknown

KEEP THE CANDLE ALIGHT

Keep the light burning
brightly between us.
Do not let me ever lose you.
One meets so few
rewarding people
in one small lifetime...
Understanding,
even though it is
for a moment,
is our only candle
against the dark
of loneliness.

—Year Unknown

THINE IS MY STRENGTH

Give me the strength to bear this pain
if it is Thy decree I must;
nor let this lesson be in vain.
Thou knowest that in Thee I trust.
I do not ask that I be spared
if pain is part of living's plan.
I know that Thou has always cared
about the joy that comes to man.
And if man is that he hath joy
how can he ever dare complain
if there are some moments
which destroy his pleasure. Joy is bought with pain.
Let me remember in this house
Thine is my strength; Thine is my power.

—Year Unknown

ADVICE

Do no complain
at present pain
nor rant about and curse
for, if you do
life will show you
it can and will get worse.

—November 23, 1996

NO DEFENSE

We can prepare for emergencies;
against most dangers we can build a guard.
We vaccinate when threatened by disease;
soft, tender skin grows calloused to be hard.
We fortify wherever we are weak.
In olden times, each cattle had its moat.
Now we excel in safeguarding technique
and every poison has its antidote.
But amours fail and one hurt has to be,
we cannot protect no matter how we try,
we must admit vulnerability.
There can be no defense against goodbye.

—Dawn. September 15, 1965

MEMBERS OF THE BORED

There is a type
of person I'm
inclined to think is irritating:
he, who insists I be on time
and always keeps me waiting!

—Year Unknown

LOVE IS ITS OWN MAGIC

Love is the magic,
the wonder,
the miracle.
Love overcomes every obstacle,
accomplishes the impossible.
Love gives strength
beyond endurance,
patience beyond comprehension,
faith beyond believing.
From intangibles,
love creates reality.
Through love, a
man and woman become as God
and create a being in their own image.
In his heart,
for his loved one,
each man builds a Taj Mahal.

-March 12, 1991

MORE YEARS, MORE TEARS

By now I've learned a certain truth
I know one fact for sure:
No matter what the faults of youth,
age is not the cure.

1988

PROCRASTINATOR'S SONG

I'm going to write. I said I would
Words didn't get me very far
I wish my actions were as good
as my intentions are.

1988

PROMISED DESTINATION

I know what good intentions do
and where they pave leads to.
The thought leaves me somewhat depressed
for my intentions are the best
but that won't help me to be saved
it just means my road is well-paved.

May 1991

ON JUDGING POETRY

If the lines are too long
and the word is all wrong;
if the rhymes sound like verse
and the meter is worse
it isn't poetry.
And if you're satisfied
with a silly bromide
with a thot that's not new
and which doesn't ring true—
then, sir, believe me:
it's not poetry.
But—
if the lines have a flair
and emotion is there—
if no technical flaws
obviate grammar's laws:
it's poetry.
And if you get a thrill
—as you probably will—
if the writing is true
and the message comes through
I'm sure you'll agree
it's pure poetry.

—Year Unknown

NO TITLE

America's reach exceeds her grasp
else what are her stars for?
Taller than the sky,
America's world is fingertip wide
and her hopes are tiptoe high.

August 1974

NEW WAY

In these days of unisex
when buying things in pairs
"his" and "hers" is too complex.
Now it's simply "theirs."

August 1974

STEPPING STONES

There is always a further horizon—
a more distant star.
There's always a challenging goal
that stretching can reach.
There's no such thing as defeat,
for wherever you are is the place to begin,
and to learn from what failures can teach.

August 1974

NECKLACE OF LIVING

Living is the golden chain
upon which are strung the glowing beads
formed by the dramatic ups and downs
of experience.
The chain is sometimes not seen
between the shining jewels
but it holds them together
and joins them at the clasp
where the beginning—birth, the first—
is slipped into the ending—death, the last—
where the first and the last
are together in one whole:
a necklace to be admired
by all who helped
to string the jewels together.

December 29, 1974

GRANDMA SPEAKS

It's not that I scorn childish joys
but must they always end in riot?
What happened to the silent toys?
Is there no fun in being quiet?

—Year Unknown

NOT BY A DAM SITE

We can't all beavers and eager to build
a dam house of mud with our tails.
In fact, there are some who, like me, are unskilled
and can't do it with hammer and nails.
Whatever I do is with tears, sweat, and blood
but at least my darn tail isn't covered with mud.

—March 1, 1990 (age 83)

LAST MESSAGE

Know this, when time comes I must leave you
with that intangible a memory,
let there be nothing in such a thought to grieve
you.
Death proves life's indestructibility.
We know that physically all things must perish.
Man cannot cling to love things that are his;
and we but build up heartache when we cherish;
the more we love, the harder parting is.
But if your heart begins to feel tears starting,
remind it, if it's missing me some night,
that ours is just a temporary parting.
I'm only waiting for you out of sight.

—November 22, 1942

FUNERAL DUTIES

TO THOSE WHO COME TO
MY FUNERAL OUT OF DUTY:
Remember, as you pass my bier,
as those who come to view, do,
that I do not like being here
any more than you do.

(Author's Instructions: Placard to be placed
above my casket at the appropriate time.)

—Year Unknown

Proverbs
by
Kathryn Kay

Strength is the fruit of humility.

o ❖ o

The highest mountain is climbed and the longest journey is traveled one step at a time.

o ❖ o

Haste and impatience bear failure but prudence and patience justify faith's vigil and bless with bounteous harvest.

o ❖ o

One small sure step on firm ground serves better than a large stride into quicksand.

o ❖ o

The fruit of knowledge is wisdom.

o ❖ o

Sufficient unto the day is the knowledge thereof.

○ ❖ ○

Without balance in all things, all is lost.

○ ❖ ○

The false step is made in haste.

○ ❖ ○

The flower is buried deep in the seed.

○ ❖ ○

Listen to naught but thine own heart and the urgings therein.

○ ❖ ○

A firm step is more to be desired that a fleet foot.

○ ❖ ○

Confusion is the start of chaos.

○ ❖ ○

In darkness the docile heart learns faith.

○ ❖ ○

Avoid the quick answer, and the seemingly

148

obvious, but ponder the long term solution.

○ ❖ ○

It is man's mistake to be trapped under the tyranny of trivia.

○ ❖ ○

Be not sparing in thy praise of work well done.

○ ❖ ○

Excess is folly.

○ ❖ ○

Safety is the fruit of moderation and balance.

○ ❖ ○

Severity must be tempered with mercy.

○ ❖ ○

Keep the door ever open for learning but embrace the new learning as a stranger, with caution, with good judgment, with great prudence.

○ ❖ ○

Deceit wears many faces, some of which are innocence and purity, even righteousness.

All joy is bought with pain.

That which bends in moments of stress will endure to stand straight again after the whirlwind has passed.

Keep supple to bend thy boughs to let the wind of adversity blow through and only the weak fruit shall be lost, the brittle twigs fall, thus making room for new and stronger growth.

Divest thyself of weightedness; thy talent is not buried. Many shall light tapers at thy candle. Thy candle is a torchlight and thy suffering a beacon. Thy strength shall be the strength of thousands.

Let thy light shine forth and go thy way in peace. Work in thine own vineyard and there will be fruit for all.

It is necessary to break new ground and break with tradition at times but only when on firm ground and when certain that firm ground is under your next step.

◦ ✤ ◦

Thy confusion is of thine own making.

◦ ✤ ◦

Too many branches weaken the strongest tree and broken branches can destroy the tree.

Good husbandry requires constant pruning.

The beginnings must be remembered and enriched so the roots may be nourished and strengthened to balance the buffeting violence of unsuspected whirlwinds which can uproot the growth of many years.

Beware of the evil lurking in the upshoot of clinging vines which can suffocate and weaken the host with their insidious sapping and draining of its strength.

Be not confused and avoid the snares of over-zealousness and the temptations which entangle.

Make haste slowly and do not break more ground than can be cultivated.

Overextension is the mother of frustration.

Much is expected from him to whom much is given, even tolerance, humility and moderation.

Thots on Public Speaking

The primary objective of a speaker is to be heard. Essential elements to being heard are:

- Overall level of volume
- Duration of syllables
- Choice and sequence of words
- Correct pronunciation of words
- Meaning of what is said

REMEMBER: For whatever you say, it's what the listener *thinks* s/he heard that counts.

Furthermore, people judge personality by voice and this is a fair judgment to be made as speech is an organically learned process.

Every part of the body used in speech exists for another purpose.

There are 4 parts of speech:
1. Motor: Lungs
2. Vibrators: Larynx
3. Resonators: Nasal/head/chest cavities
4. Articulators & Modifiers: Lips, tongue, jaw, teeth, hard & soft palates

Emphasis is determined by the flexibility of one's voice, defined as:

- Pitch (high or low tones)
- Force (loud or soft)
- Rate (speed of utterance)

Quality of speech is shaped by posture. Ideal body positioning is:

- Crown of head at highest point
- Back of neck stretching upward
- Shoulders sloping, but not rounded
- Back expanded
- Spine with slight convex curve
- Pelvis rocked forward
- Abdomen wall inward and upward
- Hands in front of thighs
- Knees unlocked and loose
- Calf muscles loose
- Heels positioned so they could press against a wall
- Body resting lightly

These are skills and positions to be practiced by anyone interested in public speaking.

Thots on Haiku

Haiku: an unrhymed verse form of Japanese origin having three lines containing usually five, seven, and five syllables respectively.
(source: Merriam-Webster)

William Wordsworth described poetry as "emotion recollected in tranquility." This is why poetry is the best vehicle for conveying aesthetic experience to a reader.

This concept is beneficial to keep in mind while writing haiku because haiku uses imagery to communicate experience—not emotions—and has been an acknowledged form of word art since the 17th century. Matsuo Basho's body of work is recognized for pioneering the style.

A proper haiku consists of three lines totaling 17 syllables—five, seven, and five syllables, respectively.

LINE 1 (5 syllables)
+ LINE 2 (7 syllables)
<u>+ LINE 3 (5 syllables)</u>
17-syllable Haiku

Haiku's concise approach to poetry requires a near-constant effort to simplify thoughts to their most basic premise.

KIGO AND KIREJI

All haikus should have both a kigo and kireji.
Kigo is a Japanese term for a word associated with a particular season.

Kireji are "cutting words" that break up the flow of the poem and allow a moment for the reader to imagine something unspoken before moving to the following thought.

The *kigo* sets the stage of an environment and the *kireji* invites imagery of action within that environment.

Haiku occurs in present tense.

In a haiku, the poet's nature and environment are one coalescence.

To this end, beware not to treat surface awareness as experience. After all, can you hear the moonlight, or listen to it reflecting on a lake?

No.

Moments of experience are naturally nonverbal. They are intuitive moments beneath a surface awareness seeking expression.

Haiku is the best vehicle to convey aesthetic experience to a reader because the world of the haiku belongs to each person alone with infinite interpretations possible.

Haikus are not just nature poems; they should suggest something nature shares with human experience because haiku *is* experience.

The *kigo* in the poem reflects this shared state of being.

Kigo words can be openly stated, but are better left implied.

Example of an openly stated *kigo*:

Full moon and the song
of the last crickets singing
in summer gardens.
-Kathryn Kay

Example of implied *kigo*:

New moon and the song
of harvest crickets singing
in resting gardens.

Although only one poem states the season outright, a moment of reflection allows the reader to discern the season captured in each scene (*summer* in example one, and *autumn* in example two). For this reason, it is common counsel for seasons not to be stated, only implied.

Remember to insert your *kireji*—the breath, or silence, within your haiku that opens the space for your reader to insert their own interpretation.

Open a space of shared experience without forcing a subjective perception.

Haikus are objective because every experience is valid.

A haiku is a pebble in a quiet pool—an expression of something boundless and endless in the present tense.

Haiku is a message that is not stated. It is as a finger pointing to the moon or the negative space in a painting that shows the least, but suggests the most.

Note from Compiler

It's been on my mind to put this book together for a while now (read: for years). Yet the idea of making a collection of my grandma's poetry available always quickly morphed into the idea of creating a perfect compilation. Which, of course, evolved into critiquing imaginary iterations while accomplishing a bunch of nothing in the real world.

Analysis paralysis took over every time I thought about moving forward and it took the insanity of the year 2020 to make it clear there was literally no point to stalling any longer. I wasn't getting any smarter on how to curate a perfect poetry selection, so I just needed to pick a concept, make sure to include some great poems (while leaving some equally great poems to be found some other way) and get a book in your hands.

Even if the book wasn't perfect.

Which, of course, it isn't.

I can name several things I want to change right now, but I gave myself the deadline of November 22, 2020, then it was time for one last read-through and to let this baby fly.

Flaws can be fixed and there can always be another collection, right?

In the meantime, the good news is that my grandma's poetry is so brilliant that it will always outshine any flaws in its setting so long as it is legible. My grandma was *that* good at stringing words together, and I aim to one day say the same of my own work and make it a family tradition.

For now, I hope you enjoyed this collection of poems from a woman who did everything she could dream up in this life before moving on to the only thing she hadn't done yet.

I hope the poems she left behind resonate and help you feel less alone in this crazy world. My grandma loved few things more than the ability of words to cross time and space to connect two people who might never meet yet understand each other anyway.

May you find that connection with her as inexplicably as the letter addressed to Kathryn Kay, U.S.A. found her nearly a century ago.

www.ingramcontent.com/pod-product-compliance
Lightning Source LLC
Chambersburg PA
CBHW070540090426
42735CB00013B/3033